T0193526

NUGGETS for ENHANCING MARRIAGE STUFF

The Little Things That Matter

MURWEEN PERRY-ROSE

authorHOUSE®

AuthorHouse™
1663 Liberty Drive
Bloomington, IN 47403
www.authorhouse.com
Phone: 833-262-8899

Published by AuthorHouse 03/25/2024

ISBN: 978-1-5462-4839-2 (sc)
ISBN: 978-1-5462-4838-5 (e)

Library of Congress Control Number: 2018907451

Print information available on the last page.

Contents

Acknowledgements... vii

Introduction.. ix

Declarative statement xi

The Beginning! 1

Marital Love Defined.. 3

Listening to Each Other.. 8

Focus 0n the Good in Each other..................................10

The Art in Apologizing 12

Speak Respectfully To Your Spouse During
      Disagreements..14

Spending Time with Each other....................................16

Showing Appreciation 18

Negotiations works in marriage....................................21

Forgiveness in Marriage... 24

Stay 'In' Intimacy... 27

Courtesies within the marriage 30

Taking Care of 'ME' in the Marriage............................ 33

Discover Common Interests as couples..........................35

Engage in Devotion 37

Communicating versus Arguing.................................... 39

Love as a Deposit or a Withdrawal 41

Be Careful of Social media Connections 44

In-laws and your marriage….. 46

Daily tips that can improve your relationship................ 49

Boundaries in Marriage.. 52

The Blaming game..55

Praying Together 57

Where are you in your Relationship? 59

Working together to be together 65

Believing in your spouse 68

How to know when your Spouse is saying, "I am
   frustrated"! 71

What does trust look like in a marriage? 74

How to be successful in long distance relationships 77

Words of Wisdom 81

Couples home and workplace testimonials 84

Myths and facts about married life 86

Know your spouse love touch 88

Helpful Bible Verses 90

The Conclusion of the Matter 92

ACKNOWLEDGEMENTS

To my beloved husband, I say thanks for his patience and time that he has allowed me to work on this project. To my wonderful daughters and son-in law, I say thanks for their unwavering support and encouragements. Special thanks to Patrice, Larissa, and Natasha for their generous support.

INTRODUCTION

This book is geared towards providing simple and valuable tips for couples as to how they can enhance their marriage by adhering to the little things that matter. After many conversations with couples as a relationship coach, and my own years of experiences as a spouse, it is my hope that these nuggets will inspire and empower couples to practice the best attributes which are vital to the enhancement of a lasting marriage. Couples are human beings first, and couples after. This implies that mistakes will be made. Growing up in different family systems and environments is unique for each individual. It also depends on the family culture, parenting styles, communication styles, and individuals' value system. These are some factors that may largely influence or impact the way a spouse may behave in the relationship. Bear in mind that some children grow up with parents who are solid examples of how to behave in a marriage; how to treat each other, how to talk with each other; how to play with each other, how to sing to each other; how to wink at each other; how to touch each other, how to kiss each other; how to walk holding hands to church, to walk down the road; or in the park, or how to hug and love each other. Others may only experience a portion of the above or none at all. The upbringing of a person can have in-depth implications for marriages. Harsh early childhood experiences can also affect a relationship in a negative way. However, as individuals grow up, there is the power of choice. Couples can learn new behaviors by re-training their brain and learning the appropriate ways to improve their relationships daily. One way to accomplish this is by applying the words of the Lord to their hearts and be willing to learn. Marriages can work if couples take time to understand each other and work on their life issues in a calm way with genuine love and respect for each other. It does take two people to show the willingness to love and care in making the right decisions. This book contains nuggets, quotations, tips and bible verses that provide some valuable instructions for all. I hope each couple will find even one tip to help them on this beautiful journey of their marriage.

Declarative Statement

2 Corinthians 5:17 states, therefore if anyone is in Christ, he is a new creature, old things are passed away; behold, all things become new. Couples will encounter challenges within their relationships for various reasons but predominantly because individuals are different. Even though couples are joined together in holy matrimony, individuals may have their own standards and moral values. It is however crucial to note that within the Christian family, couples should be new men and women through the saving grace of God as it relates to their behaviors and attitudes towards each other.

Nugget 1 ♥

THE BEGINNING!

The day of love begins with smiles and sparks in your eyes, holding hands, repeating of vows to each other, placing rings on each other's fingers and signing of the contract which states "until death do us part." Oh the joy and bliss! The wait is over. Expressions such as "I do," "I will," "I love you endlessly," and "There is no one like you," are just some of the views shared by couples at the beginning of the marital journey. You complete me, really!

The reality is that your lives together have just started and indeed you need to have those feelings, as marriage is a beautiful gift! It is important to note that along with the wedding bliss the first year of marriage can feel like the hardest because of new adjustments and changes that you and your partner will have to adapt.

Bible verse

Proverbs 3:6: "In all thy ways acknowledge the Lord and he will direct thy path".

Prayer:
Dear Lord, I pray for each couple who have decided to live together in love and harmony. Please keep them in the bond of peace and love always. For this I pray amen.

The little things matter!

Nugget 2 ♥

MARITAL LOVE DEFINED

Love can be defined as an intense feeling of deep affection that two people have and share with each other. Love can also be demonstrated in various ways depict in the following statements: Committed love, Giving love, Kind love, Supporting love, Understanding love, Forgiving love, Listening love, Silent love, Appreciation love, and Romantic love are just some of the ways to capture the essence of love within your marriage. Love is beautiful, love is kind. It keeps the heart happy and glad at all times.

Committed love allows couples to convey to each other the decision to share their life together throughout all life challenges that they may experience.

Giving love allows couples to act selflessly towards each other. This type of love stays strong through happy times, sad times, and through financial challenges.

Kind love is showing kindness to your spouse in ways that allow him/her to feel very special; whether it is through a kind word, a complement, a kind look, a kind deed, or a gentle touch.

Supporting love is being there in the moment with your spouse in all situations. It is also showing that you believe in your spouse even if a mistake was made and being the encourager in the relationship. Bear in mind that this should not be a mistake such as going outside of the marriage as this is a violation of your marital agreement, on the other hand some common mistakes which carries less pain is allowed.

Understanding love allows couples to take into consideration their spouse's imperfections. Couples will have flaws and weaknesses that will show up unplanned. This calls for patience and tolerance with each other.

Forgiving love allows couples to talk about the issues at hand or the things that are hurting each other in a mature way. Forgiving love is about making a conscious decision to release any feelings of resentment and hurt and love freely.

Listening love allows for couples to be able to be honest with each other and to share what is on their minds and also to be heard. Listening skills should be an active ingredient within the relationship. Never ignore each other when one of you is sharing your desires, your pains, your laughter, your observations, your concerns, or the news about the day. Listen gracefully!

Silent- love. Silence in marriage can sometimes be golden, but this does not refer to what is called the silent treatment in marriages. Silent in love is staying in the moment with your spouse without saying a word. It can be viewed as giving your spouse a moment to reflect on what was said and what needs to be done. It is also a moment to evaluate an action that maybe concerning and to make amends.

Appreciation love. This type of love helps couples to slow down and use I statements with each other. Some examples of these statements are, "I love you darling," "I appreciate you," "I understand," "I love you today and I love you tomorrow," "I care for you and your interest," and "I will love you always." Never take your spouse for granted.

Romantic love can be defined as a passionate form of love that couples express to each other in an intimate way. This love is more of an emotional and physical connection which draws each other closer. Creating a romantic environment will also create a deeper emotional attachment with your spouse.

- **My mother** defines marital love as a man and a woman living together, and taking care of each other in every way.
- **My own definition** of marital love is expressing love to each other in a magical and caring way.

Couples sometimes become less concerned about doing the little things that matter in their relationships because of busy schedules, lack of interest, and taking each other for granted. This ought not to be so, instead go hard at loving your spouse.

Bible Verses

I Corinthians 13:4-7

Charity (love) suffereth long, and is kind. Charity envieth not, charity vaunteth not itself, is not puffed up. Doth not behave itself unseemly, seeketh not her own, is not easily provoked, thinketh no evil; Rejoiceth not in iniquity but rejoiceth in the truth; Beareth all things, believeth all things, hopeth all things, endureth all things.

Ephesians 5:22-25 declares, "Husbands, love your wives, even as Christ also loved the church, and gave himself for it. Christ relates this type of love to how He loves the church. These verses seem to be suggesting a perfect type of love, and one may ask, "Can this be done by my husband or my wife?" For husbands, this can only be done when husbands truly love and are connected to Christ through reading the words of God for guidance and instructions. In the same breath, wives are required to submit to their husbands. This is only possible when wives' lives are embedded in the love of God. When a husband's steps are ordered by the Lord, submission is made easy for his wife. Submission, however does not allow any room for a husband to mistreat his wife in any way, but rather, being gentle and prayerful in dealing with matters. Love and submission work well together when couples' lives are entrenched in the Lord.

Prayer:

Dear Lord, Love is of you and your desire is for couples to love and care for each other always. May you grant them the right frame of mind to love each other deeply throughout the years, for this I pray Amen

The little things matter!

Nugget 3 ♥

LISTENING TO EACH OTHER

Listening to your spouse helps in opening each other hearts in showing empathy and care for each other. Listening skills are demonstrated when one spouse pays attention to what the other spouse is saying. Listening can also be viewed as the ability to accurately receive and interpret messages that your spouse would like to communicate.

Couples can know that their listening skills are active with their spouse when they establish eye contact when talking with each other, by giving a pat on the shoulder when you are not able to give an answer. A head nod or an encouraging response is also helpful. If for any reason the story the other spouse is sharing goes on for an unexpected period of time, it would be a kind gesture to express that feeling to the other spouse. Couples should develop a level of maturity to be able to say when they are tired and are unable to entertain a long conversation in that moment. Consider that your spouse cannot read your mind. When couples practice good listening, it strengthens the relationship.

Prayer:

> Dear Lord, I pray for couples to learn the art of communicating with each other but more so to listen to each other. May you give them the grace to not only listen to each other but also to hear each other. For this I pray In Jesus name. Amen.

The little things that matter!

NUGGET 4 ♥

FOCUS 0N THE GOOD
IN EACH OTHER

Focusing on the positive aspects of your spouse enhances a healthy relationship and gives a new perspective on how you view each other. Couples enter their marriages from different backgrounds with unique value systems which sometimes causes a fair deal of struggle in being your best self in the marriage. What is important though is that, couples are gentle with each other's faults and help each other to be their best self. A key factor in a solid relationship is when couples focus on each other's good habits and strengths and learning how to validate what you admire of your spouse. Always be alert and look for those un-guarded hours.

Bible verse

Philippians 4:8 Finally, brethren, whatsoever things are true, whatsoever things are honest, whatsoever things are just, whatsoever things are pure, whatsoever things are lovely, whatsoever things are of good report; if there be any virtue, and if there be any praise, think on these things.

Prayer

Dear Lord, I pray today for couples who are struggling to cope or understand why their spouse is of a certain nature. Please help couples to see the good in their spouse and pay attention to them even in the lowest moments of their lives; May you help couples to validate the positive as they grow together in love, for this I pray in Jesus name Amen.

The little things matter!

NUGGET 5 ♥

THE ART IN APOLOGIZING

Apology can be defined as an expression from an individual regretting doing or saying something that was unkind. In some relationships, couples may hurt each other and have no remorse, which is sometimes due to a lack of awareness as to how this may affect their spouse emotionally. The right thing to do as adults in a relationship would be to say, "I am sorry." When this is expressed and accepted, an apology can remove a mountain of hurt and create magical moments in relationships. It is not as hard as it seems - when mistakes are made, they should be acknowledged.

Some steps to practice:

1. Acknowledge what you did
2. Start by expressing your regrets by using "I" statements such as "I am sorry that…."
3. Take responsibility for what was done to hurt your spouse
4. Empathize and make amends sooner rather than later.
5. Be compassionate as best as you can
6. Be sincere in doing it

Bible verse

Psalm 34:13: Keep thy tongue from evil, and thy lips from speaking guile.

> Heavenly father, I pray for couples who may hurt each other sometimes with their words and by their actions. Help them to work through their issues in a compassionate way and acknowledge when they are wrong, for this I pray Amen...

The little things matter!

NUGGET 6 ♥

SPEAK RESPECTFULLY TO YOUR SPOUSE DURING DISAGREEMENTS

Couples are people with unique qualities and differences. There will be moments of variance and some flames of anger may occur. This does not suggest in any way that the marriage is over. Be mindful though that anger may not get you what you want, so take it easy. Whenever this happens, **do not** forget that you are talking to your spouse, your lover, your friend, and the person you married.

Never insult your spouse with hurtful words. Instead, highlight what the problem is even when you are angry. When couples fail to respect each other, there can be negative repercussions.

Never embarrass your spouse, especially when others are around, and neither when you alone. Neither of this behavior should be displayed among couples.

Develop the art of sharing your problems and feelings when you are with your spouse.

Do not destroy your relationship by diminishing each other. If you are experiencing challenges to say positive things in moments of despair, say, "I am not talking now" in a respectful way.

If it is possible, do not leave the home because walking away or driving away in that moment may allow the other spouse to feel disrespected, more hurt, and insecure. If you do choose to leave the home for a moment to think clearer, be careful where you go. Remember to revisit the conversation in love and with a calm spirit later before going to bed.

Bible verse

Ephesians 4:32- And be ye kind one to another, tenderhearted, forgiving one another, even as God for Christ's sake hath forgiven you.

Prayer:

Dear Lord, I pray today that couples will learn how to respect and honor each other even in the most heated moments. Please heal the broken spirits in marriages and let the words of couple's mouths be acceptable in your sight both now and forevermore. In Jesus Name I pray Amen

The little things matter

NUGGET 7 ♥

SPENDING TIME WITH EACH OTHER

The more often couples spend time together, the happier they will be. This can only be a reality if couples are being affectionate towards each other and enjoying each other's company. Couples need time with each other in order to grow and to deepen their love. Life sometimes becomes extremely busy due to work, family, and other responsibilities. Never allow your busy schedule to dictate your lack of engagement and attention to meet your spouse's needs. If for any reason you are not having fun and enjoying each other's company, it is time to evaluate what is going on and talk about it. Always remember Christ first and your marriage second, which means pay keen attention to signs of decay in your marriage.

Some tips to help:

- Plan scheduled or random dates when possible.
- Spend time together in prayer.
- Sit, listen, talk and laugh with each other.

- Respond kindly with gestures.
- Go for a walk together.
- Spend less time at friends' homes.
- Plan a surprise lunch or dinner date.
- Go to the stores, the dentist, the park, the doctor, and to the library together sometimes.
- Try to compartmentalize your life and make it worthwhile.
- If you are not an outgoing couple, find alternatives like planning a date night at home.

By spending time with your spouse, you will grow together loving and admiring each other. It will also help you to better understand your differences and how to negotiate the problems that may occur in your lives. God can be in the simplest things in marriage, just invite him and enjoy each other with GRACE.

Prayer:
Dear Lord, I pray for each couple who are struggling to find the time to spend with each other due to busy schedules, or lack of interest in each other. Please grant wisdom as to how to care so that their love can grow deeper for each other, in Jesus name I pray Amen

The little things matter

Nugget 8 ♥

SHOWING APPRECIATION

The years of togetherness in a marriage accumulated from the day both individuals say 'I do' and it continues for the rest of your life. Marriages start in single digits which develop as the years goes by into double digits. Whatever the digits are today, never stop showing your spouse how much you appreciate them. Appreciations are sometimes wrapped up in the little you do for and with each other.

Some suggestions of showing appreciation can be:

- For the years of togetherness
- For being there for each other
- For having each other backs
- For meals preparations
- For keeping the family intact

Other ways to show your appreciation:

Pay attention to each other

- Never be afraid to compliment your spouse when there is the opportunity.

- Say thanks for changing the car tires, fixing something around the house or making a meal and for helping with the cleaning or just be a good spouse.
- Express thanks for helping with the kids
- Share in your spouse's dreams, insights and plans with an open mind. Don't be too quick to say no, but make suggestions instead.
- Be patient with your spouse, none is perfect, but by reading the words of the Lord, couples can get it right.
- Keep on saying 'I love you to your spouse", this should not only be done on the wedding day; during the honey moon period, but should be reciprocate daily. It works magic!
- When was the last time you said, I love you darling to your spouse? Just checking in!!!!

As the appreciation grows, there will be some changes experience by your spouse. Self -awareness is a key factor in this situation. The young lady and young man you marry may change as the years calculated and that's okay! Changes compliments the years of marriage wisdom. This however may have some physical and emotional changes, and in addition some mood swings may even occur. If any of these become overwhelming, take a moment and share how you feel with each other. Laugh and have fun, as changes are a gift from the Almighty. In moments of illnesses or difficulties, be present, be gentle, be kind, empathize as needed and encourage each other.

Bible verses

1 Thessalonians 5:18

In everything give thanks, for this is the will of God in Christ Jesus concerning you.

Prayer:

> Dear Lord, I pray that couples will make each other their priority in everything they do, so that they can serve and appreciate each other in love, for this I pray in Jesus Name Amen

The little things matter

NUGGET 9 ♥

NEGOTIATIONS WORKS IN MARRIAGE

When you get married, you would expect everyday to be a honey moon if all possible but the reality of marriage is, there will be some type of disagreements within the relationship. When this happens couples should learn the art of negotiation and conflict resolution. Conflict is considered a normal part of any relationship, but it should not escalate to any form of injury or hurt to each other. If couples allow conflicts to intensify, it can cause a spouse to become emotionally disturbed. Bear in mind that this happens when couples do not abide by the words of the Lord, or lose focus of what is important.

Proverbs 15:1-2 instructs that **"A** soft answer turneth away wrath: but grievous words stir up anger. In other words, speak gentle to your spouse with an understanding heart. Couples can become angry but it should not reach the point where couples are insulting each other with unkind and harsh words.

Tips to work on conflicts in marriage and negotiate for reasonable solutions.

1. If and when you get angry, take time to cool off. Issues cannot be dealt with when the emotions are hot.
2. Calm down and then try talking.
3. Do not embarrass, or say unkind words to each other: Remember your spouse is your lover and your special person in life.
4. Try to understand what the other person is saying, by listening and clarifying to avoid all misunderstandings.
5. Show concern for your spouse's wellbeing, even if they are wrong, by facilitating valuable communication. This type of response can defuse the conflict and lessen the tension.
6. Find something you can agree on. No one is identical and there will be disagreements. Instead of getting mad, examine the situation and try to find things to agree on.
7. Never assume! Be sure of the facts.
8. Keep conflict under control when children are around. Remember they are watching and learning. What lesson do you want your child to learn? The lessons should be positive and not mom and dad calling each other mean names or displaying behaviors that are demeaning.
9. Try to keep disagreements in the present as past hurt can generate more pain. If something from the past is creating a disagreement, it should be

discussed only to bring closure. If there is no need for closure, stay in the present and move on with your life.

Bible verses

James 1:19- 20, "Wherefore, my beloved brethren, let every man be swift to hear, slow to speak, slow to wrath. For the wrath of man worketh not the righteousness of God".

Proverbs 14:17, "A quick-tempered person does foolish things and the one who devises evil schemes is hated".

Prayer

Dear Lord, I pray for peace within marriages. Help each couple to work through conflicts in an amiable way so as to bring honor to your name in the home and in their lives. Let right communication prevails for this I pray Amen.

The little things matter

Communication and active listening is a key factor for the success in marriages!!!

Nugget 10 ❤

FORGIVENESS IN MARRIAGE

It is a known fact that in some relationships, there is the need for spouse forgiveness. When couples hurt each other deeply it can develop into toxic un-forgiveness. Whether it was a wrong word, a wrong behavior, or a bad habit, couples need to talk about any issue that are lingering into un-forgiveness. Marriage cannot flourish with un-forgiveness. One key factor to consider when reaching out in forgiving each other is to share the hurt, the pain, the dissatisfactions, the things that you were surprised about, the things you never expected, and what makes you frustrated and sad. Never assume that your spouse knows and understand all that you are experiencing. If you are struggling with hidden thoughts, share them! The reality is that forgiveness is a key principle to live by as it more about you being free. Un-forgiveness is perceive to be unhealthy and spouse should not engaged in long months and years of un-forgiveness because as soon as there is a disagreement, the hurt is hurled out of the un-forgiveness bag and thrown at the other spouse in defense. Be mindful that un-forgiveness can lead to bitterness and resentment. On the other hand, forgiveness is healthy and can heal both the body and mind.

In a relationship, there may be times when your partner may do something that hurts, frustrates, or upsets you. When this happens, express it to your spouse say "You have hurt me," or say I did not approve of what was done, then have a conversation with the hope that the moment will allow peace and forgiveness to flow inside. The adversary is mad with marriages and he will try to plant the seed of un-forgiveness in the hearts of couples. It is of importance that couples have clear consciences and forgiving attitudes towards each other. Isn't that lovely?

Questions to ask yourself if you are un-sure of spouse un-forgiveness:

What are the behaviors' that you might demonstrate that may indicate that you haven't fully forgiven past hurts?

- What is holding you back from being kind and loving to your spouse?
- Is there something that you need to talk about or to get clarity as to why?
- Are you keeping the hurt hidden inside so as not to show your emotions or being vulnerable?
- Take a moment and think carefully of the answers, with the hope to get a clearer picture of what needs to be done to overcome past or present hurts and move towards an enjoyable life.

Bible verse: Ephesians 4:32 and be ye kind one to another, tenderhearted, forgiving one another, even as God for Christ's sake hath forgiven you.

Prayer:

> Heavenly Father, I pray for couples who are finding it hard to forgive each other. Help them to let go off any form of resentment that they may develop for each other. Please remove the burden of un-forgiveness and replace it with love and peace for this I pray amen

The little things matter

Nugget 11 ♥

STAY 'IN' INTIMACY

Marital intimacy can bring relationships to new levels of closeness. Sexual intimacy between husband and wife are the key ingredients in a marriage and this should not be neglected. It is the glue that keeps you together and an essential element of the bonding process. Intimacy does not always mean sexual relationships. An often forgotten aspect of intimacy is the emotional intimacy which is expressing your love to each other in words and having a bond. You can also express intimacy by touching and playing with each other and creating a safe space for your spouse to share his or her emotions without fear of being judged.

Some other suggestions to consider:

- Take flowers, a sweet or any other gift of love, especially on special dates is a nice gesture.
- Find out what your spouse loves and try to take it home sometimes.
- Surprise your spouse sometimes at work; take him/her for lunch if all possible.
- Serve breakfast in bed sometimes.

- Try to remember your spouse's birthdates and anniversaries and be kind and polite as possible about it. Celebrating birthdates and anniversary can be done in simple ways. It may not be the exorbitant events and gifts at all times as it is the thought that counts.

- Never allow your spouse to feel forgotten on his /her special days. Say happy birthday, or happy anniversary darling. Write a text or express a nice thought to your spouse. Know this fact! No matter who celebrate with your spouse, a husband or a wife showing that they care is extra special.

- When possible, get away for short vacations

- Write notes/text and respond to each other, it helps to keep the fire burning in the relationship.

- If one spouse is the person with the love verses, songs, or quotes, return the favor by responding with at least a word or a line. Never ignore the effort made by your spouse.

- The real energy behind a successful marriage is intimacy. When couples show each other affection by using adoring words, expressing feelings, and spending time with each other, it captivates each other's attention and love; hence, the flames of love will continue to burn brightly in your relationship.

- Keep all others out of your intimate circle, no matter the type of friendship. Let your intimate life be built around your spouse with God at the head and in the center of your relationship. Do things in love to keep your spouse home. Give the devil no chance to lead either of you astray.

Bible verses

Proverbs 5-18-19

Let your fountain be blessed, and rejoice in the wife of your youth. Let her be as a loving hind, and a pleasant roe; let her breasts satisfy you always; and be thou ravished always with her love.

Prayer:

Dear Lord, I pray for couples to continue to love and serve each other well in their marriages and to be proactive in doing the little things for each other. For this I pray in Jesus name. Amen

The little things matter

Nugget 12 ♥

COURTESIES WITHIN THE MARRIAGE

Courtesy can be defined as being polite or acting kindly to each other. The idea of only showing courtesy in the earlier days of your courtship does not depict a lasting marriage. Do you remember the days of getting to know your spouse and being the best version of yourself? There is a time and place for everything in a relationship and courtesy is one of those things to be cognizant of. There are other levels of care aside from opening and closing the door of a car. It is an everyday practice of kind deeds and good manners that adds up into a beautiful courtesy package. Couples should know what to share and how to behave in a gentle manner to their spouse in order to prevent ill-feelings in the union.

Some reminders /examples of common courtesies to practice in your marriage:

- ➢ Be kind to each other.
- ➢ Show respect to your spouse even if you are upset.
- ➢ Using the words "please" and "thank you."

➤ It is a nice gesture to greet and acknowledge your spouse in public spaces.

➤ Opening and holding the door of the car for your spouse is still a nice gesture. If it does not happen each time, just say, "Honey, please open the door for me." Your spouse will understand. Never let this interfere with your love life, just work through this with some amount of understanding.

➤ Do not allow your spouse to get lost in the hustles and bustles of a busy life and schedules.

➤ Never embarrass your spouse, instead express what you are feeling.

➤ Give a hug, a kiss or say goodbye when leaving and returning home. Never leave your home in an anger tantrum; remember no one knows the future. Say something! Or use non-verbal clues. It may not be very sentimental in the moment, but do the little things will adds up as the building blocks in the marriage.

One of the sad realities within some marriages is that, couples sometimes behave more comfortable with colleagues at work or at church rather than with their own spouse.

Common courtesy is essential for fostering a healthy relationship, maintaining love cohesion, and creating a respectful bond. Courtesy should not be a reaction but a heart attitude.

Bible verse: Colossians 4-8

Let your speech always be with grace, as though seasoned with salt, so that you will know how you should respond to each person.

Prayer:

Dear Lord, I pray your continous blessings upon each couple today. Help each one to thrive within their relationship so that they demonstrate kindness to each other by their words and actions. Let them be courteus to each other dear Lord. Courtesy is a lovely attributes which enhances the joy among couples. Please rebuke divisions and unkind habbits and grant love and peace in mariages for this I pray in your name Amen

The little things matter

Nugget 13 ♥

TAKING CARE OF 'ME'
IN THE MARRIAGE

One of the best ways to take care of your spouse and your family is to first take care of yourself. This is not always easy to do because of other responsibilities especially when children are involved. Couples should however plan a time to engage in self-care. This can be done through meditation, praying, exercise, going to the beach, reading, sleeping, enjoying moments of silence, relaxation and paying keen attention to good nutrition. It is also important that couples take care of their physical appearance, including hygiene. It is ironic that for some couples, they seem not to pay much attention to their appearance after the wedding day. This can be a great turn off for your spouse.

It would be a nice gesture to do simple things to look presentable in your appearances at home, work, social events, or wherever you may go. It helps in keeping the butterfly's feelings active and it also gives a feeling of self-validation. The fact of the matter is that self-care can transform your life and your marriage to a higher sense of intimacy. With this being said, never rely on your spouse to feel complete and whole but rather depend on the one who created you. Love yourself and take the best care of yourself. Relationships has its ups and down, so be mindful of 'Me' time.

Bible verse:

1 Corinthians 6:19- know ye not that your body is the temple of the Holy Ghost which is in you, which ye have of God, and ye are not your own?

3 John 1:2 - Beloved, I wish above all things that thou mayest prosper and be in health, even as thy soul prospereth.

1 Corinthians 3:16 - Know ye not that ye are the temple of God, and that the Spirit of God dwelleth in you?

Prayer:

> Heavenly Father, I thank you for the gift of life. I pray that couples will take care of each other and also take the time to take care of themselves physically, mentally, spiritually and emotionally. Grant each one the wisdom so that in taking care of self, the spiritual aspect will shine through for this I pray amen.

The little things matter

NUGGET 14 ♥

DISCOVER COMMON INTERESTS AS COUPLES

Couples can grow stronger together when they share similar interests. Couples should take time to learn about what each spouse loves and support each other. Sharing in common interests and fun can fill your life with laughter, grace, and mental wellness. It is okay for Husbands and wives to have different interests based on their talents, personalities and experiences.

In my marriage, my husband is a fan of cricket, football, and most recently basketball. There are times when I will watch, laugh, and scream as he enjoys one of his favorite games, even though I was not interested in all those activities. What was important is that I shared in his interest and had great fun spending quality moments together. The amazing thing that happened is that I was able to learn about some of the details about the games and I was able to have conversations about these games that actually made sense.

Some ideas of how to develop common interest and get involved in:

- ❖ Sports events
- ❖ Talent interest
- ❖ Photography
- ❖ Volunteering
- ❖ Church activities'
- ❖ Community involvements
- ❖ Art work
- ❖ Gardening
- ❖ Cooking
- ❖ Take the time to talk about childhood hobbies and find even one that you love and do it together.
- ❖ Watching TV together

Bible verse: 1 Peter 3:8

Finally, be ye all of one mind, having compassion one of another, love as brethren, be pitiful, be courteous.

Prayer:

> Heavenly Father, I pray for couples to first discover your will for their lives so that you can guide them in the process to discover each other interest in their marriage and work together in love and harmony to further bring blessings to each other on this side of life, for this I pray in Jesus name, Amen.

The little things matter

NUGGET 15 ♥

ENGAGE IN DEVOTION

Is it my belief that the family that spend time together in prayer and devotion grows together in love and harmony. Couples should take time to pray together, go to church together, read the scriptures together, and spending time in the presence of the Lord together. These are good habits for couples to develop, as they will help them to stay connected with the Lord during difficult moments in life. The spiritual element of life is essential for the marriage to grow from strength to strength. It is the key to healing, wholeness, and good mental wellness in every area of the human experience. Since God created men and women in His own image (Genesis 1:27), it's reasonable to conclude that man can never be complete without a relationship with the creator. Couples should time take out to speak encouraging words of hope, love and faith to each other as these types of encouragements can increase a level of spiritual faith within the marriage.

On the other hand, if couples are experiencing discouragement, resentment, or emotional abuse within the relationship, these can create roadblocks to spiritual closeness between partners and between individuals and the Lord. Couples should develop a daily habit that includes meditation, reading the words of the Lord and praying, and believe in the Lord for each other's salvation.

Bible verse: Thessalonians 5-11 Wherefore comfort yourselves together, and edify one another, even as also ye do.

Prayer

Dear Father, thank you for your divine love and grace. Thank you for giving couples the mind to seek after you. I pray that couples will see the need to spend time in your presence so that their lives can be deepening in your love and grace. For this I pray amen.

The little things matter

Nugget 16 ♥

COMMUNICATING VERSUS ARGUING

Communication within the relationship is like the glue that holds the marriage together for life which should be reciprocates. Communication in marriage is the ability talk and listens to each other and to know that you have been heard. Having a problem with your spouse will not disappear because you argue about the issues. It may even remain after you calm down, but approaching the problem rationally is considered a more effective way to communicate. Never ignore your spouse when he/she is trying to express a concern as this action can be seen as showing disrespect to your partner. Another important factor to consider when communicating with each other is the idea of nagging. Communicating a concern more than once should not be viewed as nagging as nagging is defined as annoying, complaining, and tormenting persistently with anxiety or pain. Nagging is not recommended in a marriage, but conversation and expression of feelings is important and should not be mistaken for nagging.

Bible verse:

Proverbs 15:1:3

A soft answer turneth away wrath: but grievous words stir up anger.

The eyes of the LORD are in every place, beholding the evil and the good.

Prayer:

> Heavenly Father, I pray today that you will help couples to develop the art to communicate with each other instead of arguing. Dear Lord please allow healthy communication to prevail and encouraged in relationships so that whatever is said will be pleasing in your ears. In the name of Jesus I pray amen.

The little things matter

NUGET 17 ♥

LOVE AS A DEPOSIT OR
A WITHDRAWAL

Love is the beginning of a beautiful journey which takes time, patience, care and a host of other positive qualities in order to build a relationship that will last to the end.

When couples fall in love and stay in love with each other they make a tremendous deposit in a positive way in what could be viewed as their love bank. On the other hand, negative behaviors can contribute to withdrawals from the same love bank. The concern though, is that for interest to grow, couples should at all time deposit good and positive things in each other love bank. It is always helpful to take a moment to evaluate what is working and what is not working and engaged in a quite discussion about the way to improve the relationship.

Some questions for reflection:

- ❖ Am I treating my spouse in a way that depicts the will of God?
- ❖ Am I loving and caring for my spouse as I should?

❖ Am I speaking health and blessings over my spouse?
❖ Am I investing in the care of my spouse?
❖ Am I admiring who my spouse really is and not only on what I don't like?

The fact is, there will always be issues within a relationship but the way they are managed determines a deposit or a withdrawal. Bear in mind! The ultimate goal is to love and care for your spouse.

Here are some checkpoints: which could be a Deposit or a withdrawal in the relationship.

☐ When couples are friends.
☐ When couples give reasons to be un-faithful.
☐ When couples make good choices which can benefit the relationship.
☐ When couples engage in anger and show disrespect for each other.
☐ When couples talk about a problem in the context of a Christian framework
☐ When couples insult and ridicule each other
☐ When couples are mean in words and actions
☐ When couples are sensitive to each other and their needs
☐ When couples spend more times with co-workers / friends /church family during spare time than with their spouse
☐ When couples spend time with each other.
☐ When couples do the little things to keep the marriage interesting.

There are various other ways in which couples can deposit or withdraw in regards to the investment in their marriage. The fact is when God is the center of your relationship; He will help you in the depositing process.

1 Peter 4:8-And above all things have fervent love for one another, for "love will cover a multitude of sins."

> **Prayer:**
> Love wonderful love the Love of God to couples. Dear Lord, I come to you today on behalf of every couple who shall read this book. I pray that couples will make that effort to always deposit in their relationships. May you give them the right frame of mind and understanding as to how to grow together in the bond of love and unity, for this I pray in Jesus Name Amen.

The little things matter

NUGGET 18 ♥

BE CAREFUL OF SOCIAL MEDIA CONNECTIONS

Couples are people who have various acquaintances and relationships throughout their lives leading up to marriage and within the marriage. These relationships might have been from childhood age, high school, college, church, work and the community. Couples may choose to connect with their friends through these medium, which can be a great idea to stay connected. There are however, the concern that individuals have changed over the years and this should be taken into consideration as to the extent couples get involved. Be aware that some friends can be very genuine about their reconnections while others can be very care-free about their behaviors which can be offensive to your spouse. For some couples, their spouse may not be the first person they have dated, or proposed to. The reality is, you both have chosen each other and the union should be respected as such. In the social media age, individuals sometimes reconnect on facebook, phones, whatsApp, Instagram and other media but this should at all times be done with some amount of transparency and decency. Couples are encouraged to be careful of reminiscing about memories that were of an intimate nature, or close bonding as this can open a can of worms. Connections and conversations like these can be unhealthy for your relationship and should not be accommodated. Couples should always be careful and be sensitive to his/her partner's feelings in this arena. It is good to have friends and associates, but be on the alert.

We are living in a world where individuals have wrong motives and couples have to be careful and avoid frustrations in their marriages. Couples should feel extremely secure in their marriages so that there is no need to feel a sense of insecurity.

"Let your light so shine before men that they may see your good work and led to glorify your father in heaven", (Matthew 5:16).

Prayer

> Heavenly Father, I come to you on behalf of couples who may get distracted in their marriage because of social media. In a time like this when social media is taking over the world and our time. I pray that couples will be wise and alert in this aspect so that no harm will be done to their relationship, for this I pray In Jesus name I pray amen

The little things matter

45

NUGGET 19 ♥

IN-LAWS AND YOUR MARRIAGE...

When couples are married, they still need their parents, their siblings and other relatives and there should be love and respect shown to everyone if all possible. There is no need for a competition of love. All can be loved at a 100% with the knowledge that love is shown in different ways and that should be respected. It is highly recommended that couples discuss boundaries within their marriage and also be careful of what to share and what not to share with their in-laws. Be aware that some in-laws may not like your spouse but the right thing to do is to be aware and share the love amidst the situation especially if you are a believer. Keep shining your light, and continue to be who God created you to be. Never allow an open door for in-laws to ruin your marriage in any way.

Some important guidelines to follow for best results with in-laws

- Try establish your own private home
- Stand up for your partner when in-laws behave in a disrespectful manner.

- Ask questions if you are not sure of a situation; never jump to any conclusions without the facts.
- If couples make the decision to live among in-laws, there should be a high level of maturity, respect, strength, and having each other's backs in all situations.
- Couples should try to be respectful to their spouse at all times and never give your in-laws the wrong idea about your partner.
- If for any reasons your parents have issues with your spouse, it should be dealt with in a mature way without any offense to your spouse or to your parents.
- Set reasonable boundaries, so that there can be peace and love in the marriage and with your in-laws.
- Never disrespect your spouse with your relatives or friends no matter the situation.
- If you chose to share a concern, be wise about it. Some in-laws can be disrespectful to your spouse, while on the other hand a spouse could be disrespectful to in-laws. This should be avoided at all times.
- If and when there are misunderstandings among in-laws, those involved should try to talk calmly without insulting or judging each other.
- When there is a disagreement, always find out the facts, don't make assumptions, ask questions and get answers. Approach the situation with grace as this is a healthy approach.
- There are spouse who maybe close to their parents than others which is understandable, but there

should be a level of caution taken about who is your first priority and allow your partner to feel that way within the relationship without any form of conflict.

- Couples should not make sexual advances to their in-laws; nor should in-laws engage in any intimate relationship with a couple.

Bible verse: Matthew 19:4-6: And he answered and said unto them, Have ye not read, that he which made them at the beginning made them male and female, And said, For this cause shall a man leave father and mother, and shall cleave to his wife: and they twain shall be one flesh? Wherefore they are no more twain, but one flesh. What therefore God hath joined together, let not man put asunder.

Prayer

Dear Lord, I pray for in-laws relationships today. I asked that you bind the plans of disunity among in-laws so that there will be unity in the family. Let every word and action be done in love, peace and harmony, for this I pray amen

The little things matter

Nugget 20 💙

DAILY TIPS THAT CAN IMPROVE YOUR RELATIONSHIP

It is said that Marriage is about "for better or worse! It is also about loving, caring working together and compromise with each other. With this being said when last you feel that tinkling in your heart, and that sparkling in your eyes when you see your spouse? (Just checking in) Have you observed that when you are happy in your relationship with your spouse, you tend to be happier with your children, your church life, your social life, which sometimes cushion all the other challenges that life may bring? When couples bond together, it creates an atmosphere of strength.

Tips that can help to improve your relationship:

- **Pray** with and for your spouse daily.
- **Say bye and greet your** partner coming home daily. This can be done in various ways such as, a kiss, a hug, a touch, a wink, or a high five, whatever you do; the key factor is that your spouse knows that he or she is recognized.

- **Send** an encouraging or supporting text to stay connected to your spouse during the day. For example, "I miss you", "I love you", "you are a wonderful person"," I am thinking about you!", "I can't wait to see you home", "Jesus loves you dearly and I love you too". These messages can definitely spice up your relationship for greater enjoyment.
- No matter how busy you are, a text or a call can take less than a minute to stay in-touch. You will be glad you did! It is also worthwhile to find out how your spouse's day is going. Share something to laugh together about and when possible, share an encouragement.
- Do things together! Go places together! This is very important.
- Think carefully before you speak
- **Show affection when out in public. Remember when you were dating and you couldn't keep your hands off each other! Keep up the good work!!**
- Encourage your spouse
- **Compliment** your partner as needed with simple words such as thanks for being there for me or thanks for checking in on me today.
- **Show** appreciation as some marriages do suffer from under-appreciation bear in mind that lack of appreciation can cause your partner to feel as if they are being taken for granted.

- Be a lover to your spouse and not just a good wife /husband.
- **Say** thanks for the little things in life. Some examples are: thanks for making dinner, thanks for washing the cars, thanks for changing the tires, thanks for picking you up from work, thanks for picking up the children from school, from games or after school programs, and thanks for having your back. Whatever that thing is, just let your spouse know that you appreciate the effort.

Prayer:

> Heavenly Father, thank you for joining husbands and wives together as one. I pray that you will rebuke the devourer who is trying to destroy marriages. Help couples to shine forth as light in their homes and in their communities.' Help them to do the things that create joy and purpose in their marriages and to keep the paradigm of love glowing and growing for these I pray, In Jesus name amen.

The little things matter

Nugget 21 ♥

BOUNDARIES IN MARRIAGE.

The Miriam Webster's dictionary defines boundary as a form of rules about what should not be done or limits that define acceptable behavior. The question is, what type of boundaries do you have in your marriage? Boundaries can also be viewed as the limit that protects the sacredness of one's marriage'. This means taking a stand to keep away all that may endanger, harm or hurt your relationship. Be aware that boundaries do not suggest controlling your spouse or taking away a spouse's freedom to socialize, instead it is more of a safe ground for safe choices within your relationship.

Some examples of boundaries in marriage:

- Be careful who you invite home, or those who are requesting to spend weekends with you.
- Be careful of staying in frequent connections with a friend of the opposite sex.
- Be careful of what you discuss with others about your spouse. This sometimes triggers strong empathy that can lead to outside relationships, or strong bonding.
- Be careful of idle feet and visits.
- Be not overly involved in other people's business.
- If someone needs help, help when you can where you can, but step back as soon as you are through.
- Never throw your mate under the bus.
- Be trustworthy and faithful.
- Be careful of opening doors for outsiders to interfere in your marriage.
- Be careful of those who bring gossip as they will take back gossip.
- Do not lead anyone on because of special attention given to that individual.
- Be careful of who you leave at home with your spouse.
- Be careful of gesticulations when taking photos with others.

Boundaries are the foundation of healthy relationships and exist to protect your marriage. They also safeguard marriages from intruders.

Prayer:

Heavenly Father, Please grant wisdom and knowledge to every couple as to how to set boundaries in their marriage in a healthy way according to your will. For this I pray in your name Amen.

The little things matter

Nugget 22 ♥

THE BLAMING GAME

Whenever couples are anxious and experiencing a stressful life they often start blaming each other for various problems in their relationship.

Placing blame about a situation on one spouse or pointing fingers does not solve any problems. In most cases, it may trigger resentment and anguish which is an unhealthy way to live your life.

One alternative approach would be to own up to your mistakes and see how you might have contributed to the issue at hand and have a conversation. Couples are not perfect people! Without God's grace, things can go wrong. What the blaming game does in a marriage is creating a stressful environment which leads to anxiety and self-protective defenses. It is important to note that there are no winners under such circumstances.

Couples do have limitations and weaknesses, which can surface within the marriage with time. Develop strategies as to how to communicate your feelings to your spouse without placing blame. Remember! It takes two people in most instances to contribute to the difficulties faced in a marriage. Love can be interpreted as a form of risk which comes with occasionally getting headaches. A better approach in expressing your feelings is using "I statements" instead of "you statements". Avoid saying things that you may regret later, and if you do, take the time to say, I am sorry sooner rather than later. Be mindful of how you communicate as your neighbor should not hear your disagreements.

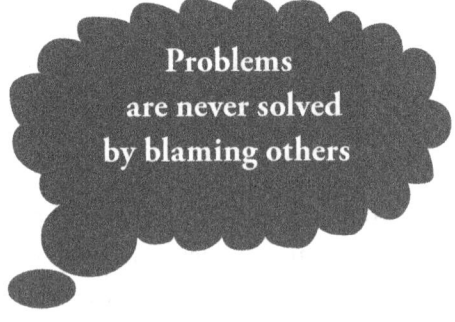

Problems
are never solved
by blaming others

Nugget 23 ♥

PRAYING TOGETHER

When couples pray together, it gives the opportunity for a better and stronger connection in the relationship. Praying together also helps in dealing with the matters at hand. Whenever you are not sure what to do when things go wrong in your marriage, it can be helpful to holds hands together and talk with the Lord or just keep on praying in your corner, the Lord does pay attention to those prayers too.

The couple's prayer

Dear Lord, We both come to you in the name of Jesus, who is our Friend, and our Savior and one who loves and cares for us. We thank you for marriage and relationships. We know you care about relationships and your desire is to see couples fulfilling your will. Help us to depend on you always for your direction and guidance. Dear Lord, we will honor you with our lives in all that we do or say. Help us to honor your words in our everyday life. Please help us to commit all our plans in your hands, knowing that you are the greatest adviser and counselor. We ask for your strength, your patience, your forgiveness, and your love so that we can demonstrate the right behaviors and qualities with our spouse. Help us to be good to each other. Help us to forgive and be forgiven when things go wrong. We will seek your strength as a shield against temptations in our everyday lives. We ask you, dear Lord to protect and watch over our relationship so that we can grow in you. When difficult times come, please help us listen and support each other. Help us to reach out and touch each other in love and never in anger. We know it is in your power to make each of us a source of your love. Let our marriage be a life well lived in you so that the light can shine forth for the world to see that we are yours by the way we live our lives. In Jesus name we pray AMEN

NUGGET 24 ♥

WHERE ARE YOU IN YOUR RELATIONSHIP?

Changes are inevitable in life and in marriages, but it is a blessing having someone to love and someone loving you back in a shared companionship. What really keeps you together? Share the answer with your spouse. Some answers that couples shared as to why they stay together are: because they love each other, for the children sake, because they are going to church, because of their religious beliefs, because they don't believe in divorce, they do not want to disappoint their parents. **The real reason for couples to stay together should be because they genuinely love each other dearly.**

Couples should be aware that amidst the challenges of life, they can survive the obstacles if they stay connected with each other. As the years of marriage grow, couples may experience various changes in their life from the "I do stage to the retirement stage". This does not by any means suggest that couples should stop trying at what makes the marriage healthy, romantic and joyful. Some stages that couples may experience are listed below:

Level 1: In the beginning

This is when couples are connected in a strong emotional and romantic way. It is a period of intense love and affection which can be describe as beautiful moments. Phrases such as, you are my darling, my sweet, my honey bunch, my lover, are typical of the initial stage. These sentiments should continue to be expressed throughout your marriage.

Level 2: The **Apprehension** stage.

This is when the honeymoon period may calm down for a while and the reality of married life starts. In this stage, couples may have to leave home early for work, dishes are accumulated in the sink, husbands/wife are asking what is on the menu, warm meals are expected and wives are asking about date nights and roses. This is a moment when couples may discover that their spouse is now a human being and not just a shining light lover.

Level 3: The **Deliberation stage**:

This is where couples sometimes start to reflect about what they have done, why they leave their parents' home, they start missing their family, friends and their freedom. Conversations may now include statements such as, what did I do? I never bargain for this", I did not plan on being your helper or why don't you do it yourself. I am ordering out for breakfast, lunch and dinner, while one spouse may say "I would like a cook meal at home." There is now the need for a conversation about preferences and how to live together and listening to each other to mitigate the concerns at hand. This stage can generate conflicts which are not healthy for your relationship to thrive.

Level 4: The **Cooperation stage**:

This is when couples develop a plan to start working together. In this stage couples may now reflect on the other levels of their lives within the marriage and note the accomplishments, the joy or the disappointments and learn to accept the fact that your spouse is your soul mate and you are enjoying each other's company. In addition, the family may now extend to being parents where couples are not just lovers but are now sharing in parenting roles. During these beautiful moments, couples' lives can become extremely busy as children now open a door for new experiences within the marriage. There will be pre-school, kindergarten, elementary, middle and high school, college, university or vocational training to be involved in. There will also be sports events, meetings and other functions after work or between work that need to be attended to. **At** this stage, couples have now realized that they are truly locked into a commitment and the only way to emerge successfully is by combining their efforts, collaborating and working as a team for things to move in the right direction within the marriage. Be mindful that this stage can prolong for several years.

Level 5: The Reunification stage:

This is another way for couples to find more time to re-discover and start appreciating each other all over again, as lovers and close friends seeing that children may now be in college or living on their own. Let these moments be splendid, fulfilling and enjoyable. You both deserve it.

Level 6: The Life changer stage:

In this stage, there are various changes that couples growing together can discover; for example emotional, physical, mental financial and Career changes. When these changes occur, one way to be successful is to tap into the compassion for each other and communicate.

Other life development changes that couples should bear in mind as they grow and develop together are the idea of midlife crisis, Menopausal, Andropause and Retirement stage.

- ❖ There are various thoughts provided by researchers describing midlife crisis as an emotional period that men and women go through between the ages of 35/60. Some individuals may have an early experience rather than later on. Male and female may encounter some un-comfortable experiences which may result in significant mood swings, change of behaviors' and acting out behaviors.
- ❖ Transitioning to menopausal stage is noted to be the end of a woman's reproductive years which allow for women to sometimes experience various intense feelings. Being aware of some of the common signs will help couples to go through the most difficult time with a level of understanding.
- ❖ Men on the other hand may go through andropause stage where the male hormones may decrease. Some

of the expected symptoms range from feelings of fatigue, isolation, low or high sex drive, low energy depression or sadness, decreased motivation and difficulty sleeping.

In these moments the way to honor each other is to care more, love more, play more, demonstrate your spouse love touches, be gentle and exercise patience with each other on a daily basis. It is also very important to stay in-love and maintain a solid friendship. Couples can enjoy every moment of this stage with grace, understanding, gentleness, kindness and pleasure.

Some recommendations that can help in navigating your way through these moments are:

- Couples accepting that these changes are happening and recognizing that changes are a normal part of life.
- Be your spouse best friend
- Hang out together and enjoy each other's company.
- Talk about your individual changes that you are experiencing, laugh, love, cuddled up and express your true feelings.
- Be there in each moment with each other.
- Engage in self-discovery learning on the topics for more understanding.

Another life development to consider is the retirement stage: couples can sometimes face intense challenges or stress related issues in their marriages when there are no plans in place for this stage of life. It is recommended that couples actively prepare for this stage of their lives as without a plan there can be high levels of frustrations within the marriage.

Questions to consider for this transition:

- Is there a permanent home?
- Are there any savings account?
- Are there any retirement or burial plans available?
- Are there any plans for vacations
- Are there any plans for your children?

Prayer:

> Dear Lord, I pray that you will grant couples an understanding heart to support and work with each other in the various stages of their life. Let the Holy Spirit be the eternal force for which each couple will rely on to keep them in the bond of peace, long lasting love and harmony amidst life challenges. For this I pray in Jesus name Amen.

The little things matter.

Nugget 25 ♥

WORKING TOGETHER TO BE TOGETHER

When two people marry, they take vows to be together for the rest of their lives. This can only be achievable when both individuals genuinely love each other.

Marriage covenants are meant to be permanent until death, but this does take some work from both individuals staying committed. (Romans 7:2-3). Take for example a marital vow which states, I promise before God my family and my friends, to be your loving and faithful husband/wife, to live with you in health, wealth, and sickness and forsaking all others, as long as you both shall live. This is just an example of the types of vows that couples may say to each other. Taking marital vows often includes the entire package of the one they marry. This is a promise that should not be taken lightly especially by believers. Working together to be together is the honeymoon period all the way to the end.

Workable suggestions to help in staying together:

- Love each other

- Take care of yourself
- Invite the Lord to take precedence in your relationship.
- Keep a private home.
- Be honest with each other.
- Live within your financial means the best way you can.
- Never dwell on the past, talk gentle about problems and forgive.
- Be kind to your spouse in your words and actions
- Keep all negatives words and actions out of your marriage
- Speak words with positive inspirations to your spouse.
- Be sensitive to your spouse's feelings and needs
- Never place your children in the middle of conflicts. It is okay for them to know that disagreements will happen but they should observe and know that you both love each other, no matter what the situation is at hand.
- Be careful of selfish behaviors' in the marriage
- Take care of each other's hearts and needs
- Live, laugh and love daily; enjoy every moment
- Develop a daily money management within your budget the best way you can.
- Be mindful of self-care
- Give compliments to your spouse in public and private places.

1 Corinthians 7-10-11 advice couples to make all effort to remain in their marriage.

Prayer:

Dear Lord, I pray today for your divine help for every couple to work together in love and unity, so that they can stay together for life. Let peace and understanding prevail in their relationships. Where there are hindrances let there be reconciliation. Grant them wisdom, knowledge and understanding in all they do for this I pray in Jesus name amen.

The little things matter

Nugget 26 ♥

BELIEVING IN YOUR SPOUSE

Believing in each other can be an affirming perspective which can leads to a satisfying marriage.

The story was told of a Christian couple who had been serving the Lord for many years; unfortunately, his wife lost interest and gave up on serving the Lord which affected their marriage immensely. Her husband never stops believing in her and in the Lord for his wife salvation. When she would express her thoughts about stop serving and working for the Lord, he was like the energy that kept her going. He kept on reminding her of her love for the Lord, her testimony, and her dedication in the service of the Lord. The situation took some time to resolve, but her husband kept on praying to the Lord for his wife to be fully committed again. In the end she testified that it was God and the faith that her husband showed in her helped her to bounce back. His wife finally was able to reconnect with her master and has been working and serving the Lord ever since. The logic behind this story is, "Never stop believing in your spouse whether it is for your spouse's salvation, for a job, for a change of heart, for healing, or for deliverance. Always remember there is nothing too hard for God to do (Jer. 32-27)

Tips that can help in being the "Believer"

1. Make your marriage your first priority
2. Believe in each other and trust the process
3. Read the words of God constantly and be an encourager in your marriage.
4. Treasure and pay attention to your marriage
5. Be watchful **and stay in the words of the Lord for** the adversary is working on his techniques to separate the family. When the family is broken, the home, the school, the church, the community and the society at large will be broken down.

Believing in yourself will give you a deeper sense to believe in your spouse

Prayer:

Dear Lord, I pray for the believing spouse within each marriage. I pray that each one will seek after you for strength when they feel weak. Help them not to give up on each other in bad times. Comfort the hearts of those who need your guidance in moments when they are discourage. Let them be a channel of blessings for your glory. For this I pray in Jesus name amen

HOW TO KNOW WHEN YOUR SPOUSE IS SAYING, "I AM FRUSTRATED"!

Couples who start out loving each other sometimes find themselves stress because of difficulty that they are experiencing to the point that they end up feeling frustrated in the relationship. It is important that couples pay keen attention to the signs that may indicate when a spouse is saying they are not happy, they are at a breaking point, or they are tired of the lack of attention and the inconsideration shown. When these signs are evident, couples should take some time to communicate this to each other in a caring way. If matters are unresolved, spend some time in praying about the issues at hand or reach out for professional help.

Some signs of frustrations:

- When your spouse is not smiling.
- When your spouse wears a frown most of the time.
- When your spouse is more interested in talking with others than with you.
- When sleeping position changes from head to feet.

- When you nag until it pains the heart.
- When you continue to accuse each other without the facts.
- When a spouse behave thoughtless
- When your spouse is always angry
- When couples are together and there is total silence most of the time.
- When a spouse stop touching each other.
- When your spouse seems emotionally numb.
- When your spouse is not interested in taking a walk with you.
- When there are no fun times together.
- When conversations are held in tones of anger.

If any of these conditions is happening in your marriage, take some time to reflect, evaluate, talk and try to re-build your relationship and love again. When there is joy in a marriage, one does not need to light a candle to see, it will naturally radiate in the little things you do with and for each other. Never take your spouse for granted.

Prayer

Dear Lord,
Thank you for the medium of prayer. I pray for couples who are struggling to meet each other's needs and are now feeling frustrated in their marriage. Help them to rekindled true love and compassion for each other. Help them to forgive where forgiveness in needed. Heal their marriages for this I pray in Jesus name. Amen

The little things matter

NUGGET 28 ♥

WHAT DOES TRUST LOOK LIKE IN A MARRIAGE?

Trust is a fundamental factor in a marriage. It is like the energy on which a marriage flourishes. With this being said, trust can be viewed differently for each couple due to principles and family dynamics. In a conversation with some couples, they described trust as being faithful in good and bad times, being transparent, setting expectations, honesty, no cheating and having a deep sense of security in their relationships. This type of assurance provides a safe net within the marriage. When there is a lack of trust, there is also a lack of integrity that invades your marriage which can open the door of relationship doubts. Talking about your concerns is recommended with the hope that trust can be rebuilt and restore with time. Bear in mind that trust is a key factor in building a solid relationship.

Tips that can be helpful:

1. If you are aware of any behaviors' that depict distrust, talk about it immediately.

2. Make a decision to forgive where necessary, take some time to evaluate the situation and pray for the courage to work through the issues if all possible.

3. Couples should acknowledge that mistrust has consequences.

4. Be transparent

5. Communicate truthfully.

6. If you are hurting share your pain, with the hope that the other spouse will respond.

7. Be honest and listen attentively to each other with your heart.

8. Renewal of vows happens for various reasons in marriage; this could be one of the reason in which couples can rebuild broken trust.

Prayer:

Dear Lord, I pray that couples will live their lives in such a way that trust will be elevated in their relationships. Grant them wisdom and knowledge to be self-control and to develop necessary boundaries in all that they do and say for this I pray in Jesus name. Amen.

The little things matter

Quotes

1. It is hard to trust someone who does not trust themselves.
2. There is no halfway in trusting 'trust should be all the way.
3. Trust comes with faith, hope and expectations.
4. Trust does not needs muscles, it just need a heart.

HOW TO BE SUCCESSFUL IN LONG DISTANCE RELATIONSHIPS

Long distance relationships are said to be challenging, but can also be an incredible experience when couples communicate and plan well. When couples sign the agreement to say "I do" with plans to live separately for whatever the time period maybe, an immediate plan needs to be developed which can solidify the relationship through distance. In a conversation with individuals who are committed to their spouse in long distance relationships, shared that it has its advantages and its disadvantages but the best way to enjoy precious moments is to stay closely connected.

Some tips to consider and practice:

- Develop an active plan for connecting with each other and keep the line of communication open at all times.
- Have a working phone.
- Work quickly on living together, if at all possible
- Create your own pattern of how communication will be done on a daily basis.

- Believe in your marriage and in your spouse with the faith that your relationship will be successful.
- Set up your preference of communication for different events and activities in your lives for example: birthdates, anniversary. Via, text messages, emails, telephone calls, video calls, snapchat or skypes or a visit. The key point here is that these preferences must be agreed on by both parties to avoid any frustration or anxiety.
- Be trustworthy, transparent and honest with each other. If there are any concerns with your relationships, talk about the situation, but never assume or judge without the facts.
- Prioritize talking with your spouse amidst your busy schedule as this is the major ingredient that will break or make the marriage
- If there are feelings of insecurity or jealousy, discuss it in a respectful way and clear the air.
- Be careful where your mind will lead you in lonely moments. Always think positively, and when in doubt, pray.
- Create some agreements that both spouse will honor.
- Engage in humor sometimes.
- If a spouse is from a different culture, this should be discussed with a level of maturity as to how to maintain the relationship. Identify things that you are concern about and present a workable plan which should be respected.
- Talk about financial issues and put a reasonable plan in place.
- Stay away from nagging each other.

- Be careful of involving third parties in your relationship.
- It is important to give each spouse time as there are the conditions of work life and other engagements to take care of.
- Never be the boss of your spouse even if you are the one with the financial stability in the relationship.

Maintaining a relationship takes love and dedication from both parties. When couples lives thousands of miles apart, keeping a healthy marriage can become much more challenging when there is a lack of understanding. Couples should develop a workable plan as to how to stay in-touch with each other in amiable way.

Prayer

Heavenly Father, I come to you on behalf of couples who have engaged in long distance relationships. I pray that you will guide them as to how to relate to each other with kindness, honesty, transparency, and care. Bind them together, dear Lord as chain that cannot be broken. May your holy spirit intervene in their marriages. Let no evil come nigh their dwellings. In times of distressed, let them feel your presence near them. For this I pray in Jesus Name amen.

The little things matter

Bible verses of encouragements:

For he said, "The LORD watch between you and me, when we are absent one from another. (Genesis 31:49)

Fear not, for I am with you; be not dismayed, for I am your God; I will strengthen you, I will help you, I will uphold you with the right hand of my righteousness (Isaiah 41:10)

NUGGETS 30 ❤

WORDS OF WISDOM

➤ **"Relationships** and marriages can be ruined when one person continues to learn the simple rules of marriage; while the other person holds on to their old habits.

➤ Spending time validating your love for each other will help the relationship to grow stronger.

➤ It is never recommended to go to bed angry with your spouse, instead express your concerns.

➤ Do not expect perfection from your spouse as it does not exist.

➤ There may be days when you may not like each other or may not want to be around each other, but during those moments, remember the love that brought you together.

➤ Engage in marriage evaluations and assess what is going okay, what could be different and what could be improved and together develop a workable solution.

➤ Never yell at each other. Keep it fair when there is a disagreement and show some class. Unkind words spoken can be forgiven, but they can never be taken back.

> Pay some attention to anniversaries, birthdays and any other special occasions in your marriage. These events help in creating beautiful memories which can be treasured.

> When you get married, stay married.

> "It's okay to fall in love more than once with your partner.

> When you get married, reflect on the person you marry, and the person you will allow your spouse to become in the marriage.'

> Make an effort to treasure the good in each other; do not mess up each other's lives. If you are not managing well, seek professional help.

> Keep a list of the good experiences and discard the bad ones

> "Be aware of your anger and the tantrums that follow. It can ruin the joy and bliss of happy moments.

> "Couples with children should be aware of their behaviors at all times, as the way they love and treat their child's father or mother could be teaching their sons and daughters how they should treat others or how others should treat them.

> Couples should not ignore their spouse intimacy and sexual needs without a discussion.

> Never think badly about yourself when your spouse speaks down to you. It is never about you!

> Life is brief! Criticize less, fight less, quarrel less, complain less, love deeply and love hard.

➢ Always take into consideration the now! Do not waste time with the past, the assumptions and the negatives.

➢ Each day, give thanks for each other, speak health and blessings over your spouse and enjoy your life together.

➢ It is inevitable that the high level of intimacy may slow down over time but what is helpful is to be honest and talk about the issue and develop [new ways of keeping the romance alive.

➢ Never bully or shame your spouse to get submission; to submit becomes easy when the head of the home is at a good place spiritually.

➢ Make an effort to go on dinner dates or on vacations sometimes.

➢ Communicate as a grown up

➢ Never lose your own value system

➢ Love your spouse from beginning to the end.

NUGGET 31 ♥

COUPLES HOME AND WORKPLACE TESTIMONIALS

When couples are at work their roles and responsibilities are completely different from that of the home and this should be understood by each spouse. There is however the concern for some couples where their partners may demonstrate a more contented behavior at work rather than what is portrayed at home. In a conversation with some men, they reported that their spouse keep a nagging home which makes them feel uncomfortable at home on most occasion. This can be painful, but the thing to do is to talk about what may be the reasons for this type of behavior. To enjoy a healthy relationship at home couples should discuss what they want instead of allowing home to feel like a place of nagging.

While nagging is not recommended in a marriage, having a conversation should not be seen as nagging but more about engaging with each other and providing the necessary feedback. Life at home should depict wholesomeness which will automatically shine through at work without being judged.

Tips that can be helpful:

1. Check in on yourself on reflect on what could be done differently at home.
2. Never showcase how much you care, love and share only at work when home is not taken care of.
3. Never pretend or wear a mask to be a great person at work but a weak person at home.
4. Be true to yourself wherever you go.

Prayer

Dear Lord, I pray for couples who are struggling to be transparent and genuine in their behavior both at home and at work. I pray that you will grant them the wisdom needed to honor each other and to be true in their actions in Jesus name I pray amen

NUGGET 32 ♥

MYTHS AND FACTS
ABOUT MARRIED LIFE

Marriage is a commitment and should be honored as such. All may not be exactly as a spouse dreamed their marriage to be but with faith in God and true love and affection relationship can thrive.

Examine these statements and determine whether they are facts or myths about marriage. {F or M}

- My spouse needs to know what to say to make my marriage happy at all times.
- When I become a parent, my spouse will be closer to me.
- There will be no disagreements in my marriage when I am happy.
- Marriage completes me in every way.
- When I find my Mr. Right or Mrs. Right, all will be well in my life!
- Happy husband! Happy bonding!
- Happy wife! Happy life
- I will be happy once when I get my wedding ring

- I can control him/her as soon I get the ring
- If I am rich, my relationship will be awesome
- If I do everything right, my spouse will love me
- Couples must have similar professions for their marriage to work!
- When I get married I will change him/her into the person I want him/her to be!
- Money is what makes my marriage works!
- Living with in-laws enhances my marriage!
- Living with in-laws can affect my marriage in a negative way!
- Spending time with your spouse in prayer is essential!
- Honesty is the best policy in a relationship!
- When couples prays together, it helps to sustain a pleasant relationship.

Nugget 33 ♥

KNOW YOUR SPOUSE LOVE TOUCH

A love touch is that extraordinary touch that couples can utilize to get closer and stay connected with each other for life. It is therefore essential that couples learn the 'touch' that speaks to your spouse emotional needs. A gentle touch from your spouse works like magic in the relationship.

Below are some tips that can helpful

- A touch on the shoulder can be done in the form of a tap or a squeeze.
- Sometimes a tickle can be irritating but if that is your spouse's love touch, play and have fun.
- While sitting or standing beside each other, a touch every now and then gives a good feeling.
- A rubbing of the hands or gentle touch on the palm speaks volume in the bonding process.
- Taking a walk holding hands together is an adorable gesture.
- A hug is one of the colors that can increase the romantic page of the relationship.

Touch plays a crucial role in enhancing love. Take a moment and reflect on the days when you could not keep your hands off each other and just do it all over again.

NUGGETS 34 ♥

HELPFUL BIBLE VERSES

Genesis 2:24 - Therefore shall a man leave his father and his mother, and shall cleave unto his wife: and they shall be one flesh.

Proverbs 18:22 - Whoso findeth a wife findeth a good thing, and obtaineth favor of the LORD.

1 Corinthians 13:4-7 - Charity suffereth long, and is kind; charity envieth not; charity vaunteth not itself, is not puffed up.

Ephesians 5:25- Husbands, love your wives, even as Christ also loved the church, and gave himself for it.

Proverbs 21:9 - It is better to dwell in a corner of the housetop, than with a brawling woman in a wide house.

1 Corinthians 7:39 - The wife is bound by the law as long as her husband liveth; but if her husband be dead, she is at liberty to be married to whom she will; only in the Lord.

Matthew 5:32 - But I say unto you, that whosoever shall put away his wife, saving for the cause of fornication, causeth her to commit adultery: and whosoever shall marry her that is divorced committed adultery.

1 Corinthians 7:3

Let the husband render unto the wife due benevolence and likewise also the wife unto the husband.

Colossians 3:19

Husbands love your wives, and be not bitter against them.

Nugget 35 ♥

THE CONCLUSION
OF THE MATTER

Marriage offers a remarkable opportunity to live a selfless life. To love and fall in love over and over again, to cuddle and laugh, to be intimate with each other, to communicate, and to embrace each other and most of all to stay in the will of God. These are just some of the things that complement a marriage. There has not been a research, or a story about a marriage without some type of challenges. Never destroy your marriage over the little stuff that you may not able to change instead, take the little things that matter into consideration and appreciate each together. There are many resources on marriage including this book, but the Bible is the major source of instruction as to how couples can engage in a successful relationship. Loving your spouse as yourself conquers selfishness and conflicts.

Philippians 2:1-5 "If there be therefore any consolation in Christ, if any comfort of love, if any fellowship of the Spirit, if any bowels and mercies; Fulfill ye my joy, that ye be likeminded, having the same love, being of one accord, of one mind. Let nothing be done through strife or vain glory;

but in lowliness of mind let each esteem the other better than themselves. Look not every man on his own things, but every man also on the things of others. Let this mind be in you, which was also in Christ Jesus".

If for any reason you are struggling as a couple and you are not sure of what to do, please reach out to a professional counselor, a relationship coach or a pastor for support as needed.

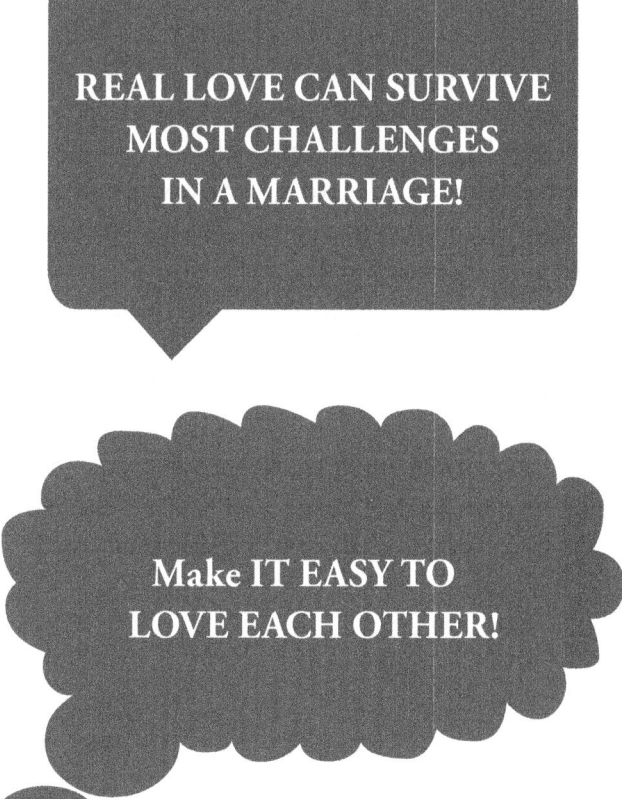

REAL LOVE CAN SURVIVE MOST CHALLENGES IN A MARRIAGE!

Make IT EASY TO LOVE EACH OTHER!

Who will this book help?

The nuggets for enhancing marriage stuff; offers some profound tips with a spiritual focus to help couples to consider the little things in life that matters which can create a loving and lasting relationship. These nuggets are based on some real life experiences of couples who are struggling in their marriages. No one enters into a marriage with the thought that they are going to failed or divorce each other but the records of failing marriages' are of concern. Each spouse chooses their partner for a reason with the intention to live lovingly though good times and challenging times. This sometimes gets loss in the buzz of life which for some couples they forget to stay focus of what is most important (each other). Too often a marriage is destroyed only because of the little things that are left un-done and are taken for granted in the relationship. It is the hope of the writer that couples will find even one nugget in this book helpful and will serve to help in rekindling hope, joy and love in their relationships.

If you are experiencing any marital problems that has become overwhelming. Please reach out for professional help with a certified counselor or a relationship coach.

<u>The five helping C's for couples</u>

MURWEEN PERRY–ROSE is a member of the counseling profession, a Certified Relationship Coach and a Motivational Speaker. She is also a Prepare Enrich Facilitator in Pre-Marital and couples counseling. Murween is a wife, and, mother and serves in her church as a minister. Her motto is "If she can help one person at a time her living will not be in vain".

Printed in the United States
by Baker & Taylor Publisher Services